Help!

My anger controls me

Introduction

Anger – an emotion we feel towards a person, thing, or situation when we believe that we have been wronged or hurt in any way. We often view it as an emotion that brings nothing but negative things, though deep down we know that it only ever causes damage when it is uncontrolled. If you feel that your anger happens frequently in various inappropriate levels and you know that your anger causes you undeserved stress, this book is exactly for you.

With this book you will be able to:

- Appreciate yourself and the others more by understanding how anger happens
- Meditate like a pro at home or at your workplace with just 5 minutes to spare!
- Know the secret to being the bigger person by forgiving without reserve
- Perform constructive ways of releasing anger in a way that's beneficial for you
- Learn how to properly reflect in writing, which helps a lot in knowing yourself and how your anger affects you

- Take complete control over your emotions, thereby grasping the secret to how to be calm in times of frustration and how to end anxiety

In other words, this book is great way to hone your control over your emotions, allowing you to manage anger effectively by staying calm. This book is actionable for both workplace and home setting and in your personal relationships.

Together, let's take a pause and reflect on our emotions and in particular, anger: what is it, what does it do to us and the people around us, and how can we reign over it.

Table of Contents

Chapter 1 – The Anatomy of Anger: Why your anger is different from mine

Anger is an emotion that drives a person to dislike or antagonize another person, a thing, or an event because he feels like this has done him wrong. Like the other emotions that we have, such as sadness, fear, joy, and excitement, anger is different from individual to individual. This difference happens because not all of us get angry for the same reasons and our anger are not always on the same level; moreover, we also express our anger differently. Let me give you a very personal example:

The first time anger picked my curiosity was when I was in college. Don't get me wrong; I get angry from time to time, but there wasn't a moment when I stopped to think about this feeling that drives me to make rushed decisions – until that one fateful day in college. That time, our professor tasked us to write a paper about a relevant social issue that we can relate to as students. For some reason he also moved the deadline ahead, only notifying one of the students in our class whom we shall call "Keith". Unfortunately, Keith failed to inform everyone; sure, more than half of the class was able to submit on time, but the others – including me – missed the deadline and got lower scores. While some of my classmates blamed Keith, berating him for his "lack of concern" and "irresponsibleness", I merely stood and accepted the scores. This is when I got curious: imagine rendering hours to accomplish a task and not being able to receive the grade you deserve because a person failed to inform you of the moved deadline! I understand why some of my friends were furious, but why can't I bring myself to get angry?

Let's see: what Keith did affected me the same way it affected my other classmates, so the right thing to do is be as angry as them, right?

Wrong.

This is what I would like you to understand about anger – we might experience the same thing, but we might also react differently depending on how much the situation triggered us. Just like in my personal example: the lowered scores didn't trigger me the way it triggered my other classmates, so our reactions are different.

Another interesting thing is that anger can be unpredictable: you see, our brain has two portions: the cerebral cortex and the limbic system. The first is the "thinking" part, involved in evaluation and judgment, while the limbic system is the "feeling" part. Within the limbic system is the amygdala, the part which collects all the happenings around us. It will also be the one to decide whether a happening should be sent to the cortex or to the limbic system. If the situation conjures strong emotions, the amygdala will override the cortex, sending it right away to the limbic system. This is what we call as "amygdala hijacking". Once this hijacking takes place, a surge of hormones will occur, prompting us to a fight or flight response.

Let's have an example:

My friend, Edgar is one of the most reasonable people I know. He seldom gets angry and when he does, he's still so calm and collected, listing down all the things he disliked about the situation and talking peacefully to the person involved. So, imagine my surprise when Edgar punched a co-worker while we were having a lunch meeting! Now, I'm not going to discuss why Edgar got so angry, but the gist of it is that on the times when he was calm and collected, the thing that made him angry do not summon enough emotion to bypass the cortex. When he punched a co-worker without so much as counting to three, it's obvious that the amygdala hijacking took place.

So, you see, one can never truly assume a person's reaction. We do not know what angers them and we won't know just when the limbic system will take over. As a summary, our anger is different from one another because:

- We react differently to "triggers". The trigger comes from either physical or emotional origin and our reaction to it might be affected by past experiences. And since we have varied life experiences, our reaction to the same trigger may be different. You can be nonchalant to a certain scenario, while I may already be fuming in the inside.

  Example Scenario: Alice grew up in a household where food is scarce, that's why she gets angry with her daughter whenever she doesn't finish her food. Michelle on the other hand grew up with a controlling father, so when her son doesn't finish the food, she lets him be.

- Sometimes a scenario doesn't bring about pain, but because we are bombarded by another emotion, we become angry. Remember that most of the time pain alone cannot make you angry. It is when pain is combined with other negative emotions that we feel anger boil within us.

Example Scenario: Anna, a mother, loves answering her child's questions no matter how repetitive or trivial they are. But on times when her husband shouts her misgivings to her, she becomes intolerant of her son's questions and often lashes out on him. Here we can say that Anna doesn't get angry with the questions – it's just that she becomes intolerant of it because another emotion (hurt) is bubbling inside her.

- The pains include both emotional and physical. This is why people who don't feel well are quick to get angry.

Example Scenario: A patient suffering from pain will get angry easily, that's why nurses are trained to understand and empathize with their situations.

- At times, people get angry – either unconsciously or intentionally – to divert their attention from a much more painful feeling. You can say that people are sometimes using anger as a "distraction".

Example Scenario: I would much rather get angry at a person for "stealing" my best friend's attention than accept that my best friend likes her better than me.

Now that we know how and why anger is different from person to person, it's now time to understand how this is important:

- It will make you understand yourself better: what situation angers you? Why do they anger you?
- It will make you understand others better, allowing you to be more tolerant of their burst of anger.

And these two, understanding yourself and understanding others, will ultimately give you the ammunition to control anger because you have more knowledge on how to manage the triggers on your side and you will be more compassionate of the scenarios involving other people.

The Takeaway:

Biologic processes, like production and release of hormones, take part in how often and how severe we get angry; however, other emotions and feelings brought by our life experiences also play important roles.

Chapter 2 – Why Anger is Good and the 5 Questions You Have to Ask to know if you have Anger Issues

Anger – like all the other feelings that we encounter – have both the positive and negative effects. Most of its effects are motivational. For one, releasing anger helps us calm down, refreshing our minds enough to be able to look at the situation with renewed perspectives. Another is it pushes us to do better: for an instance, being angry that we have been looked down on will inspire us further to achieve our goals so as to get the recognition we deserve. Additionally, being able to reflect on one's anger is a sure-fire way to notice if an injustice is happening. And finally, let's not forget that anger is often used as a temporary distraction, keeping us grounded when we are at our worst.

Still, we should not forget that all these benefits cannot be reaped if what we have is uncontrolled anger. When unmanaged, anger can only lead to increased anxiety and higher risk of depression. It also severs previously good relationships because of hurt feelings and rushed decisions. Lastly, anger affects our health – our heart, lungs, and even sleep cycle are unknowingly harmed!

So... for this chapter, this question remains: **how do we know when our anger is uncontrolled?** This is harder to answer than we can imagine because angry people almost always feel that they have the right to get angry. In other words, they seldom see reason at the height of their emotions. Additionally, those with anger management problems often do not take the time to reflect. To determine the problem, someone has to talk to them OR they must reflect on times when they feel better. Whatever the case may be, answering the following questions will help ascertain if you (or someone you know) have anger issues:

1. *How often do you get angry?*

    If you answer daily, proceed to the next question because there might be a slight chance that your anger is warranted. If you say several times in a day, that's already a red flag! People don't get angry that often! Also, ask: how long does my anger last?

2. . *Why do you get angry?*

    Reflect on the reasons why you get angry. If you get angry because of small and accidental things, you might have anger issues. However, if the nature of your job involves supervising people, with some of those being constant headaches, your anger may be justified. The bottom line is to think: Is my anger proportional to the current situation?

3. *How are your relationships with other people?*

    Notice how people act when they are around you: do they feel comfortable in approaching you or do they purposely avoid you? Ponder on your friends: are they still inviting you over your weekly dine-out, or you're already excluded?

4. *When was the last time you tore up or broke something because of anger?*

    Anger often drives us to throw or tear something. If you often experience this, there could be anger issues involved.

5. *When was the last time you said and did hurtful things?*

    Uncontrolled anger often makes the person say and do hurtful things; sometimes, they even become abusive. What was the last cruel thing you said to anyone? Have you physically hurt someone recently? Or was there a moment when you were so close to hurting someone? If you can affirm these situations, you need to start managing your anger; otherwise you and the people around you will continue to suffer.

To be fair, answering affirmatively to these questions doesn't necessarily mean that you are hopeless. In fact, if you are still at a point in your life where you can identify the need to get better, half of the battle is already won. Some people who have anger management issues need medical attention, but others simply need to take a break, reflect, and try things to alleviate the problem.

The Takeaway:

Not knowing when we have anger management issues is a huge stepback; one will not be able to solve a problem without knowing that a problem is existing. Once you know that you need a little guidance, that's half the battle won.

Chapter 3 – The Life-Changing Benefits of Managing Anger

Once you have ascertained that you have anger issues, you need to recognize the reasons why you need to control them. In general, controlling your anger and mastering your emotions will be good for your overall health, but to be specific, here are the life-changing benefits:

1. Opens better communication lines. When you don't shout at people or throw random objects, you maintain an open communication line. This will make you understand the situation better and will appreciate why the person is trying to do what he's doing.

2. You'll be able to make better decisions. If you can't think clearly out of anger, you'll regret whatever decision you

make. Deciding while angry often results to rushed actions, such as physically hurting someone or verbally assaulting a person.

3. With open communication lines and better decision-making capacity, your relationships will be closer and healthier. This is because your loved ones will not be afraid to get close to you.

4. Significantly reduce you stress. Constant and uncontrolled anger is often a heavy burden that causes stress; with you being able to master your emotions and knowing how to end anxiety, you live a less-stressed daily life. And this will not be only good for your emotional well-being but also for your physical health.

5. Become a more likable person. A person who's always angry isn't likable and will probably not win any favor, big or small. In any profession, authority is needed but likability is also essential. This is good for a harmonious relationship with your colleagues.

I know that you'll agree: achieving these benefits will totally improve your life not just at home, but also at work. The effort you'll put into mastering your emotions will be all worth it if you'll obtain these treasures.

Chapter 4 – 3-Step Rule to Easily Master Your Emotions and 5 Effective Ways to Take a Pause and Gain Control

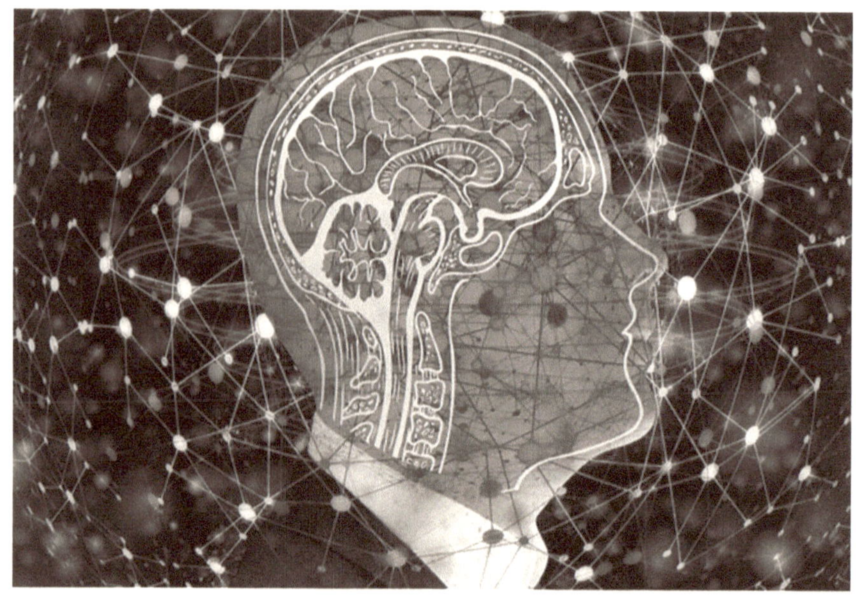

Being able to master your emotions is a great way to control, if not totally prevent anger. But, is it possible to truly master one's emotions? If you're thinking around the spectrum of always being in control and never getting angry, then the blunt answer is NO, but if you're along the lines of managing your feelings and actions particularly in tensed scenarios, then YES, we definitely can be masters. Mastering your emotions will not only encourage you to be calm – it also has the power to end your anxiety.

So how do stay calm during the time of anger? You simply follow this program:

Step 1 – Feel the emotion before it overcomes you.

The first step to control your emotion is to actually know when the emotion is there. Take me for example, when I am angry, I tend to snap at the person I am currently angry with. I scowl and make sure to let that person know why what he or she did is unwise. I don't stop until I am sure I got the point across. *I didn't even know I was angry until after I did the act!*

To master your emotions you must know when they are present. This is also an essential key on how to stay calm. Not knowing what's happening will prevent you from employing the strategies in this book, so you need to focus on this first. Overtime, this technique will be an effective weapon against uncontrolled anger.

But how will you know when the emotion is coming to you? You can look for the following signs:

- Increased heart rate
- Headache and stomach ache (as anger sometimes manifests physically)
- Sweating, especially on your palms
- Shaking or trembling
- Feeling warm or hot around your neck and head
- Grinding your teeth

- Clenching your fist

Some people will not notice that they are angry because they fail to pay attention to their body; they just feel the anger, and in unfortunate times, they will just act out because of it. Knowing when the anger is there is a great edge to think more before doing anything.

Step 2 – Remember who's in control. YOU.

Once anger is realized, you must instigate your control.

Remember that famous line: *No one can drive you crazy unless you give them the key?* Well, emotions work that way as well. An important step is to understand and accept that while your anger can come from external triggers, the last command will come from you. You must be worried: wouldn't it be like bottling up our emotions? Isn't that a bad thing? Well, first things first: bottling up – or totally repressing your emotions – is really bad. Think of yourself as a bottle and your emotions as soda. As life happens, the bottle gets filled up and if you don't release them, the contents will overflow. When the bottle is shaken (think, intensive situations) the emotions might explode. Good thing our 2nd step is not about bottling emotions – it's about controlling it. Control means not acting without thinking, even at the height of anger.

Before we proceed, let me tell you that controlling your emotions are easier said than done. If I have to describe it in one word, I would say TRICKY. Come to think of it: people with anger issues often do not get to assess their feelings – they jump right into action, without thinking, without reserve, nothing! The result is embarrassing at best and damaging at worst. You can lose friends over hurtful actions and sharp words.

But, how do you regain control after knowing that the anger is there? Sometimes, people count to ten, but most of the time, they aren't enough. Listed below are some of the things you can do to control your anger:

1. Pinching a pillow or the cushion you are sitting on; this is especially a good technique if you are in a meeting or in a conversation which you cannot cut

2. Counting backwards, very slowly (start from high numbers such as 100)

3. Go out and drink water; this is a good excuse to get out when you have a private or group conversation

4. Pinch on bubble wrap

5. Splash your face with cold water

As you can see, most of these activities can be used to get out of a sticky situation, so it won't be difficult to incorporate them. While doing these things, ask yourself: "How did it happen?" "What's happening?", "Why do I feel it?", "What am I doing?"

This way, you will have the leverage to know if the anger is too much or when it's just appropriate. The more you pause, the more you'll see the logic behind what happened.

Step 3 – Decide on What to Do Next

Let's have a little recap: when faced with a frustrating situation, the first thing you'll do is be aware if you are angry, the next is to take a pause to control the anger, and the final step is to decide on what to do next. Generally, you have 3 choices:

1. Let things slide. If you got angry because of a petty thing like a lost scissor at work or your son drinking straight from the pitcher, perhaps you can let things slide, especially if it happened for the first time.

2. Talk to the person or people involved. If you feel wronged and if you think that it won't stop until you speak up, talk to the people involved calmly. Be objective. For an instance, if you are angry because someone in your family keeps on "forgetting" to do his chores, sit him down and say that you don't like that his chores are almost always done by someone else. Try not to bring up past transgressions as that will only unnecessarily make things more complicated.

3. Follow HR procedure. If a co-worker angered you and you know that what he did is against a policy, take it properly

to appropriate channel. Follow the protocol. You may be sat down with each other, but that it better than mindless confrontations. Of course, please know you can also not take the case to HR; you can simply approach the person involved.

These are the steps to take for when you are in the actual situation, but you can perform better in controlling your anger by doing these three things: preparing a trigger bank, meditating, and understanding that your anger isn't you.

Get Ready, Prepare a Trigger Bank

Do you remember how it feels like to review for an examination? If you do, then you are probably familiar with questions bank. These are the collection of questions that the department might give based on what you have learned. The more you practice on those questions, the more you will feel comfortable in the actual questions. With this, you become more confident in taking the exams.

In mastering your emotions, you also need to prepare a bank, but instead of questions, it'll have your triggers. Triggers are the happenings, scenarios, occurrences, that give you emotions. In this particular step, you need to identify the triggers that set off a very loud emotional alarm. The things that make you "lose control".

Let me give you an example: with her permission, my good friend, Kate, shared two of her triggers in the bank:

1. Hearing that others' projects are better than hers

2. Knowing that she is being purposely left out

Kate said that when these two happens, she couldn't focus on the task she is doing; she's annoyed, hurt, and angry all at once, making her snap at the people involved. By "snapping", she means answering their questions sarcastically or downright being mean to them. According to Kate, listing down the triggers and already predicting her reactions help her contain the bubbling anger by either "adjusting" the feeling or totally manipulating the situation. Adjusting the emotion means doing Step 2 – the only difference is you do it even before the scenario actually happens. Manipulating the situation, on the other hand, means being proactive; for an instance, if you know that your trigger is being left out, do something about it by asking some questions!

To prepare a trigger bank, have a base list ready. Get a notebook and write down the things that make you angry. Opposite the list, think of how you can remedy the situation or how you can control the anger. Here's an example from Kate's list:

1. Hearing that others' projects are better than hers – try to see how my project can be better; learn from that project

2. Knowing that she is being purposely left out – proactively ask questions; understanding that I cannot always be included in things

Understand that your reactions are NOT you

Now that you have your triggers and the possible actions, you need to understand another thing: reactions are – most of the time – a spur of the moment happening. You didn't think about it. You didn't know you were going to hurt anyone. And most importantly, you didn't like whatever negative thing that happened later on. In other words, the reactions you have to the anger you feel do not reflect you as a person.

You may be a little off in controlling your emotions, but you have a good heart. This alone will make you feel better and when you feel better, you will handle your emotions more properly.

Meditate

This step is "less confrontational". You see, meditation can be done even if you do not feel any negative emotion, such as anger. Every day, regardless of your mood, is perfect for a quick meditation – you don't need to sign up to a class, or to be seated perfectly still because this activity can be personalized. To help you, please refer to the following guidelines:

1. Allot at least 5 minutes daily; meditating need not be done at the same hour each day, especially if you'll only need a few minutes, so finding a break time is not really an issue. The key in making this habit regular is to turn a routine activity into a signal – something that will urge you to meditate right after. I, for one, meditate after drinking my afternoon tea; a friend of mine who is working in a law firm meditates each time a meeting is adjourned. How about you?

2. Choose a place of meditation. While blog articles and magazine covers suggest the place to be green, serene, and peaceful, your meditation venue shouldn't follow the hype. The general requirement is for it to be safe, have minimal distractions, well lighting, and ventilation. The aesthetic part is just a bonus. Think: in what part of the house are you safe and comfortable? At your work place, what could be your meditation venue?

3. Decide on the kind of meditation you want, mind you, there are a lot! To name a few, we have walking meditation, seated meditation, Zen, mindfulness, visualization, body scan, and transcendental. While I cannot give you a play by play of what each entails, I can tell you that whichever you choose will help you take better control of your emotions.

4. The premise behind meditation as a tool to master your emotions (and thereby control anger) is called "mind

stilling". We get angry because we feel powerless and we don't do too well when we are not in control. Doing meditation regularly will help us understand that we have choices and we always have the ability to choose. Let's see: say you came from a week-long conference, you are sleepy and hungry and you plan to doze off in flight after a hot meal. All of a sudden, the airline staff said your flight will be delayed and you need to wait for another 16 hours! You intensely dropped your baggage as a show of protest, screamed at the staff, and posted bad words online about the service.

5. Doing regular meditation will help you realize that none of those actions magically gave you a private jet to get you to your destination on time. It'll also make you more open to choosing other options; in this case, you could ask the staff if they can offer any sort of compensation, like a free meal or hotel accommodation. If they don't, you can take the time to have the extra 16 hours to yourself – see the places, take a bunch of selfies, visit a restaurant, among others. The point is, you have a lot of options other than to act out on your anger. Mind you – it is not necessary for you to suppress your anger, you just need a better way to handle it.

Meditation will help you.

6. Transition yourself into the routine. A simple mindfulness meditation starts with a relaxed position (seated is common). Once comfortable, find your breath: this means focusing on your breath; notice the rise and fall of your chest as well as the passage of air in your lungs. Don't bother if you are breathing too fast or too slow, too deep or too shallow – those things don't matter because as you accept your breaths as they are, they will even out. As you focus on nothing but your breath your mind stills – there are no worries, no anger, nothing! Think of this as an emptying exercise which refreshes the mind. When you're done, slowly reorient yourself in your surrounding before ending the session with a simple prayer or a short sentence of gratitude.

7. For a mindfulness meditation, instead of just focusing on your breath, you can also focus on the things that are currently happening: the hum of the air-conditioning unit, the footsteps down the hall, the temperature, or the feelings of your body. Mindfulness means you are appreciative of the "here and the now" – not the past, the future, or any other place, that's why you can do it whenever and wherever you are. If you're eating, be mindful of what you are eating. If you are doing a task, be mindful of that task. You can do it even when you are walking, granted that you are safe in the area.

Meditation works like a mind-break; sometimes, when we think too much, we become incapable of deciding rightly and we act in rush. I suggest having 5 minutes daily for this activity – you won't see the results right away, but in a few weeks, you sure would!

The Takeaway:

When faced with a situation that angers you, you have three steps to take: know when you are indeed angry, control your emotions by pausing for a bit, and decide on what to do. Additionally, you can be better in managing your anger by preparing a trigger bank, knowing that you are not your actions, and by meditating. These are also essential steps to take on how to stay calm and how to end anxiety, which are good for your holistic health.

Chapter 5 – Remove the Roadblock: How to be the Bigger Person

Often times, our anger happens as things around us happen. A co-worker says some hurtful words, a trusted loved one failed to protect you, we are rejected, a situation got us so insecure, etc. In this instances, when we release our anger, it's done and over with. The feelings may stay a little bit longer, but we can talk to the people we once got angry with.

However, there are also times when our anger came from deep seated, unresolved situations. And in this case we remain angry to a person even when he is not doing anything to us at the moment.

I'm saddened to say that if you have not yet forgiven the person who wronged you, the three-step strategy we discussed in chapter 3 won't work. If we can't forgive, then our mind is closed. For an instance, even when anger comes to you, you won't care. You also won't take a pause. And your decision to hurt the person is already made up.

In other words, if you still haven't forgiven the person, you will feel like it's alright to get angry.

If you are someone who harbours deep-seated anger inside you because you cannot forgive a person, let me tell you that you will have a harder time in managing your anger. No matter how much of what we have discussed in the third chapter you accomplish, you will still end up angry because you cannot let go. Your mind is closed and you feel that you can do anything else OTHER than to forgive your aggressor.

That's why this chapter is included. It's time to be the bigger person and forgive! And you can do it in just three steps, which are:

Step 1 – Accept that the event that caused the anger already happened. There's no taking it back. No matter how angry you become or how much you detest the person that caused it, it still happened. Should this anger inside take any more of your happiness? Wouldn't it just make things worse?

Step 2 – Accept that the person who wronged you is not perfect. Perhaps he or she did it intentionally with the purpose of hurting you or lifting his or her status at your expense – everyone is flawed, after all. Maybe he just feels insecure that he has to put you down or perhaps he really didn't want to hurt you but he succumbed to the desire of being better. What he did is unfair, but who knows what's he's going through when he did what he did?

Step 3 – Accept that you learned something from the experience. You might have developed some trust issues after what happened, but be honest: you also became smarter. There's always a silver lining even to the most painful of situations.

Once you appreciate these things, it will be easier for you to forgive. More so if you learn that forgiveness…

1. Is something you do for yourself. Not for others. Not even when they are pressuring you to do it.

2. Doesn't mean you have to forget. Take the event with you, but don't begrudge it. Learn the lessons and move on.

3. Will not require you to be best friends with the person who wronged you. The truth is you don't even have to include the person in your life and you're not required to inform him that you have already forgiven him!

4. Means you will still have feelings about the person or the event. The only difference is these feelings will no longer act like shackles around your heart. It means you can still feel sad about it and you are definitely allowed to talk about it.

5. Never excuses the behaviour of the person who wronged you. At no point should you feel like you're "encouraging" the wrongdoing simply because you have forgiven.

Generally, once you have forgiven, people shouldn't challenge you to meet the person AND you are never required to rise up to that unreasonable dare. Forgiveness is just between you and your feelings. If you feel the need to tell the person about your newfound freedom, go ahead; after all, whatever his reaction is will not affect the fact that you have already forgiven him.

Once forgiveness is achieved, you will feel tons lighter than before and it will be easier for you to handle your emotions, particularly your anger. Not only that but you will also improve as a person – a bigger person, at that.

The Takeaway:

No anger-management strategy will work if you cannot forgive. There are a lot of things people misinterpret when it comes to forgiveness, one of which is the idea that once you have forgiven someone, it means the end. Forgiveness is a long process, but it is worth it because the benefits you will reap are deeper than any anger or pain you feel.

Chapter 6 – When things get out of hand: 4 better channels for your anger

When you perform the 3-step strategy along with trigger bank preparation, meditation, and forgives, one of the two things may happen: the first is your anger eases, and the situation which started it is rectified. This commonly happens for scenarios which you can change, one-time mistakes, and fleeting situations. The second thing that can happen is your anger eases, but the situation doesn't change. Let me give you an example:

A coworker of yours always gives out offending remarks. Take note, he's not exactly a bully, so you can't take it to HR, but it seems like he always wants to provoke you, especially when you're down. You constantly do the 3 step-strategy and most of the time, it works. But your strategy isn't his, so you're the only one who's changed. He is still the same person who likes to provoke you and sometimes he's just too much! What will you do then?

And this happens not just at work, but also at home! Your kids are different from each other and you use different strategies to handle them the best you could, but that could be exhausting. Your husband or wife can be a little too much from time to time. Chores may pile up because of emergencies and a change you experience may not be always for the better.

The bottom line is, sometimes things will go out of our control. They will make you angrier than usual and the 3-step strategy will only help a little, but not totally, so you'll need to release the anger in a beneficial manner.

Naturally, you'll have to release your anger, but not in a destructive manner.

To help you channel your anger in a beneficial manner, please refer to the interesting list below:

1. Play ball sports. Instead of throwing objects or hitting people, why don't you hit the ball? Sports such as tennis make it easier for you to hit without hurting an object or a person. Not only is it a good release, it is also good for being physically fit. What I also like about tennis is you can do it anytime, with just the ball, the racket, and a sturdy wall.

2. If your anger can wait a little bit, you can also resort to other forms of release such as hitting a punching bag or throwing the ball to a wall and catching it. Swimming is also an option, as well as running or jogging. The point here is to engage to only solo sports or release activity, especially if you don't want to be around people when you're angry.

3. Dance. Dancing, believe it or not, is a very effective way of transforming anger. After sweating and releasing a lot of breath, you will feel tired but definitely refreshed. If you're lucky, you'll fall asleep right after and wake up to a better mind set. The best thing? Dancing can be done alone in your house with just the music busting from the speakers or your ear buds.

4. Visualize. Here's one interesting thing about anger – you can still release it to the person involved... but only through your imagination. This is called the gestalt strategy. In a normal setup, you can place a chair in front of you and express your anger. You can scream and all, if that will make you feel better. An alternative version is to visualize the person – no props needed. Go to your room and walk back and forth; think of the person you are angry with and tell him or her exactly what's on your mind.

5. Please remember that this strategy is mostly done for an anger that has been kept for so long. Still, you don't need to wait until it gets to that point. You can do this technique right away even when the anger is just minimal.

6. Take a walk. Meditate. When you're angry and you feel like it will overcome you, take a walk. If it's not enough, you can meditate. Walking meditation is a little different than seated meditation in the sense that while you are meditating, you still need to keep an open eye and mind on the happenings around you. To start, you need to pick a place with a safe, good walking path. Make sure that the path is long enough, either straight or circular. Avoid a path where there are changes in directions because we want to limit the need to make decisions. As you walk the path, think about your anger, where it came from, and what you can do about it. This can take around 5 minutes, give or take, but it can do a lot for your anger.

The Takeaway:

The strategies to control anger and master your emotions work like magic but you still cannot have total control of the happenings around you. At times, things will become too much for you to handle that anger and frustration will make you feel like you'll explode.

Don't self-combust. Release your anger through the steps listed above.

Chapter 7 – The Best Answers to the Uncommon Questions You Might Have

Each of us has a specific problem we wouldn't like to admit to anyone but badly needed answers for. Here are 5 of the most common, yet unspoken topics, about anger management issues and the corresponding answers which effectively solves them.

What to do with a privileged co-worker who passes her work to me?

No matter where we are, we always encounter privileged people who feel like it is our obligation to follow their orders, so the first step to solve this problem is to see if his actions are solely directed to you, or he's like that with everyone else.

If it's with everyone else, then it doesn't need an intervention on a personal level. This means you can simply start gathering evidences that he made you (and the others) do the work for him and then take it to HR. If it's personal, then you need to take the same steps as earlier, but when you go to HR, you need to mention that he's only like that with you. Take note that while the steps are similar, the intervention will probably be different.

My mind goes blank, I shake when I get angry

Don't worry, it isn't uncommon to experience this, so you aren't alone in the situation. If your mind goes blank, let it go blank. Don't be pressured to respond to the situation right away. Take a pause. Reflect on what happened. And when things come to your mind, sort them out. Reach out to the person with a clear mind. Don't fall into the trap which says that you need to say the winning "punch line" right in the heat of the moment.

When you're shaking, find a release, like what was suggested. Throwing a stress ball at the roof top is also a good release as well as a way to clear your mind.

My mom and I both have anger issues and it's tearing us apart

This is bothering in the sense that you are already being torn apart because of anger issues. If the problem is at this level, it is highly advisable to approach someone who can counsel you and your mother. Have a common person accompany you to a counsellor and start the healing process there.

Road Rage

Road rage is pretty common, especially for people in stressful jobs who still need to take roads with heavy traffic. The first advice is to never go driving if you're already angry about anything. Let the feeling pass first. Next is you might want to take the longer route, but one with less vehicle traffic. While driving, turn on some calming music. And one of the most effective ways: be kind on the road.

If the rage comes to you, don't get out of the vehicle right away. Collect your thoughts for a few minutes before tackling the problem, and as much as possible, have someone else out there when a confrontation happens.

Abusing my puppy and I don't know why...

"Abusing" is such a strong, negative word here, so the first thought that comes to mind to deal with this is for you to at least not have pets for now. It's not a long term solution, though, so don't worry. The first question I want to ask is: when do you abuse your puppy and how? Are you hurting the pup in any way, like depriving him of food and water, hitting him, or leaving him out in the cold? Why? Are you stressed at work? Are you looking for something to receive your anger? If yes, then have someone else take care of your pet for the mean time. Address the anger issues first with the strategies discussed in this book, especially the one where you release your anger in a constructive manner.

If anger isn't the problem, do you think you just don't really like having pets? If this is the case, no one is forcing you to have one, so you can think of asking someone else to adopt the pup.

Chapter 8 – Anger Management Worksheet

As a final chapter, let me ease you into this worksheet. The truth is, you can consider this as a "check in page": you just need to use the same questions over and over and answer them daily, or every other day – as long as you regularly attend to the questions and tasks below. I want you to do this because I realized that in the course of my journey in anger management, checking in worked like a therapy. And it's not only me! When I talk to people about it, they also affirm its effectiveness. Please note that some of you may like journaling better and that's also okay because this worksheet also acts as a journal, albeit a little bit more structured.

The instructions are simple: you can use a blank notebook or notepad, whichever you prefer, and write a couple of things on top: particularly, the date, day, and the general status of your emotions. Are you happy? Sad? Angry? Or so-so, meaning you're okay – no emotions in particular are bothering you. If you've written any other emotion other than angry, you may proceed with free journaling, meaning you are not required to answer the questions below. On the other hand, if you've experienced anger - or anything close to anger - during the day, proceed with below:

1. If you can rate your anger, with 10 being the angriest and 1 being the least, what will be your rating?

2. What caused this angry emotion?

3. Were you able to control it? How? What happened after? Were you happy with the results?

4. If you were not able to contain your anger the way it should be contained, what was your reaction? What was the result? Are you happy about it? If not, what would you have done differently?

5. Now that the milk has been spilled, what's you next step?

6. After answering these questions, go over the emotion wellness checklist below and tick it if you have already done it for the day:

   • Have you spent a few minutes of silence? Have you meditated?

- Did you have breakfast, lunch, dinner and snacks in between?
- You've done something good today! Did you do something to appreciate it?
- Talk to your closest friends or colleagues about something funny and light
- How about offering a simple thank you to something good that happened?
- Also, offer a thought of gratitude for something bad that taught you a lesson.
- What of yours have you given today?

I know that this list is short compared to what you have in mind, so go ahead and add a couple of things in this list! The more personalized the better!

Bonus! Routines you need to have in a daily, weekly, and monthly basis...

...To be able to master your emotions and control anger!

Daily

- ☐ Take small breaks
- ☐ Eat healthy meals, on time
- ☐ Have a good laugh over lunch
- ☐ Meditate for at least 5 minutes

- ☐ Take a walk
- ☐ Write down on your journal
- ☐ Do as many kinds things as you can
- ☐ Be thankful

Weekly

- ☐ Treat yourself (go to a movie, buy a book, etc.)
- ☐ Go back on how the whole week has been by reading your journal entries
- ☐ Make a gratitude letter to include in your prayer

Monthly

- ☐ Go on a relaxing trip alone or with friends and take time to meditate while traveling
- ☐ Look back on the whole month and be grateful for it

Conclusion

You can never banish anger: it's a natural emotion that's bound to come to you from time to times, especially when you are vulnerable (when you're tired, unwell, frustrated, hurt, etc.) What you can do is to control your emotions and manage anger. And we can do that using the strategies in this book which can be summarized into:

- Understanding that anger is different for everyone, thus you must take time to get to know yourself and others, so that you'll be more tolerant of the anger coming from them and yourself.

- Determine if you have anger issues by asking the questions listed in Chapter 2; and appreciate what anger management can get you in Chapter 3. These will make you more determined to learn how to stay calm and manage your anger.

- Control your emotions and learn how to stay calm by performing the three-step strategy which are:
  o Know when your emotions are there by feeling for the signs
  o Take control of your anger by taking a pause and getting busy as you reflect
  o Decide on what to do

- Additionally, preparing a trigger bank so as to anticipate your reactions and meditation also help.

- Meditation helps to refresh our perspectives; you can perform meditation daily for just 5 minutes

- Forgiveness opens your mind to the strategies listed above; if you cannot forgive, you wouldn't care about getting angry; in fact, you may even feel that it's okay to be angry.
- When things become too much, you need to release anger in a constructive manner; not destructive
- And finally, reflect on your day. This will not just help you master your emotions, it will also end anxiety.

Last but not the least; don't forget to practice the steps. Whenever something in your work life or family life angers you, perform the three essential steps, mediate daily, reflect on your trigger banks, forgive, and release anger whenever needed. Also, don't forget to accomplish the worksheet in Chapter 8.

If you feel like things are really too much for you to handle, please never hesitate to approach a counselor or someone who you trust to bring you to a counselor. Asking for help isn't a dead-end. You might be surprised as how it will open up a world of opportunity for you to conquer your anger and master your emotions.

Managing anger is an investment and you will be surprised at how the returns will change your life!

Sincerely, Adriana Hutsell

www.ingramcontent.com/pod-product-compliance
Lightning Source LLC
Chambersburg PA
CBHW051128250726
48655CB00007B/2953